The Great Catch of Fish

Luke 5:1–11 for children

Written by Lisa Konzen
Illustrated by Ronnie Rooney

Simon and Andrew fished the lake
Of Gennesaret all night,
But not one fish would their nets take,
So they gave up the fight.

They washed their nets and stowed their gear
As crowds along the beach
Were gathered 'round so they could hear
The words that Jesus preached.

The crowd pressed close to hear His word.
What message would He give?
His words were fresh; they'd never heard
That in Him, they could live.

Then Jesus spotted Simon and
He asked to come aboard.
He told him to row out from land,
And Simon obeyed the Lord.

They listened to Him preach Good News
As water lapped the shore.
When He was done, He told them to
Row out a little more.

"Go out in deeper waters and
Let down your nets; you'll get
A catch of fish so big and grand—
Your best night's fishing yet."

Then Simon said, "We've fished this lake
Without a single bite
But for You, Master, I will take
Another try this night."

They rowed away despite their doubt—
The fishing wasn't great.
They dropped their nets and looked about
But didn't have to wait.

The catch was big; their nets began
To burst and fall apart.
They called to every fisherman
To come and do his part.

The boats began to tip and sink,
The catch was so immense.
It really made poor Simon think
That Jesus' words made sense.

He knelt by Jesus and said "Go
Away from me, my Lord.
I'm sinful and I didn't know
To take You at Your word."

"I didn't trust when You said, 'Fish!'
That I'd find perch or trout.
You gave me more than I could wish.
Oh, Lord, forgive my doubt."

Then Jesus said, "Don't be so scared.
I have a job for you.
So listen up, and be prepared
For what I call you to."

"You see those folks along the shore?
Like fish, they're swimming 'round.
They know life must have something more
Than what they've always found."

"They're looking for a Savior who
Will die to make them free.
I'll give My life, make all things new
So all can live in Me."

Like Simon, we must drop our net
And help those fish inside.
You won't believe the catch you'll get
When in Him, you abide.

Dear Parents,

Simon had worked hard all night and had nothing to show for it. Nevertheless, the exhausted and defeated fisherman obeyed an illogical command from an itinerant preacher. As a result, Simon and his partners were rewarded with incomprehensible success. What they netted was beyond their wildest imaginings. What they netted (besides a lot of fish) was forgiveness and eternal life.

Simon was well aware that he was a contemptible man in the presence of the holy God. Hopelessly tangled in the net of his own sinful nature, he fell to his knees in the smelly, dirty bottom of his boat and said, "Depart from me, Lord, for I am a sinful man."

"Don't be afraid," Jesus told him. "Follow Me." Forgiven, Simon was now ready to respond to Christ's call to serve in the world. He let go of the nets that bound him to his sinful life and put his faith in his Lord.

This event marks the beginning of the advancement of Jesus' ministry on earth—the commissioning of His apostles. This advancement continues today as pastors are called to preach the Gospel and administer the Sacraments and believers are called to gather in His Word and around the Sacraments. Like Simon, we confess our sinfulness, kneel in His presence, and receive His forgiveness for our sins.

In addition, the story of Simon Peter's great catch of fish mirrors the great conversion of thousands as they listened to his sermon on Pentecost. Simon had indeed become a great fisher of men.

The Editor